MW01070199

Understanding Iran™

IRAN
and
IRAQ

RELIGION, WAR, AND GEOPOLITICS

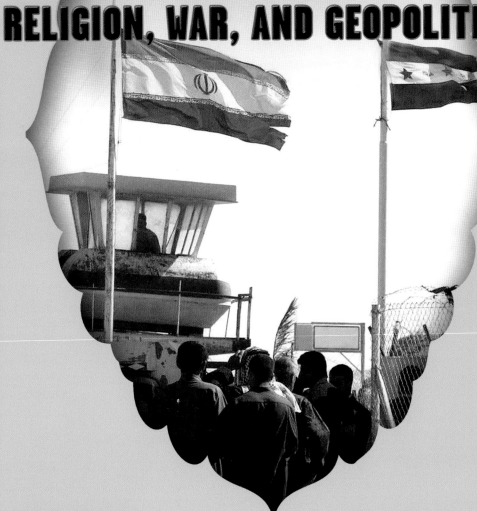

ROSEN
PUBLISHING®

New York

Philip Wolny

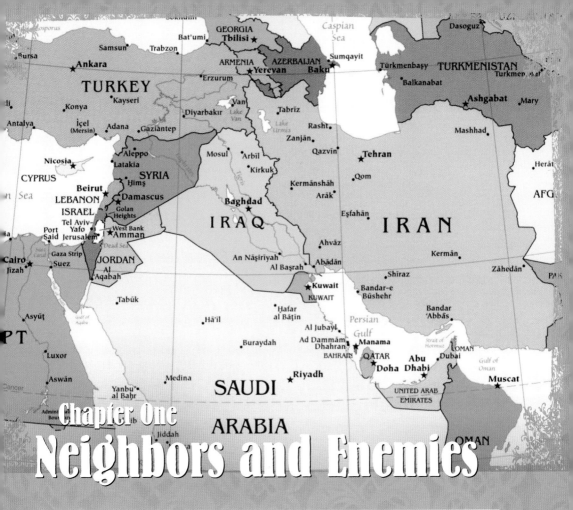

Chapter One
Neighbors and Enemies

I ran and Iraq share a long border. They also share a complicated, sometimes bitter history. Centuries before the modern era, and before the existence of Iran and Iraq as nation-states, the people dwelling in these lands were in conflict. For example, the Persian Empire was centered in what is more or less present-day Iran. The Persians had frequent border disputes with the Ottoman Turks, who for centuries controlled what is

Iran and Iraq, oil-rich powers in the Middle East, have long fought over their border regions and access to the Persian Gulf, the vital shipping channel they both depend on.

now Iraq. Relations were further complicated by religious differences. While most people of both these lands were Muslim, they each practiced differing—and frequently opposed—branches of the faith.

When Islam first rose in the seventh century CE, it spread from the Arabian Peninsula. Islam would later split into two dominant sects, Sunni and Shia. The split occurred because of a dispute over who would lead the faithful after the prophet Muhammad, its founder, passed away. Much of what is now the Arab world, including Saudi Arabia, Egypt, and Syria, is predominantly Sunni.

When Islam spread to the Persians, they initially adopted the Sunni faith. Eventually, however, most of Persia began to practice Shia Islam. Hence, while the region is predominantly Muslim, there remain significant religious differences between the mainly Sunni Arabs, who long ruled Iraq, and the mainly Shia Persians, who dominate in Iran. The differences are not only religious but cultural, too. For example, Iraqi Arabs, whether Shia or Sunni, hail from a tribal society. On the other hand, Iranians have a long tradition of urban society. In addition, the sophistication and splendor of pre-Islamic Persia is as important as Islam to Iranians' sense of history and identity.

Much tension also arose due to the historical divide between the two Muslim-majority nations. Iran was overwhelmingly Shia (90 percent of the population). However, Iraq's population has been mixed, with the majority Shia (about 60 percent) living alongside a sizeable Sunni minority. In addition, there are the

Kurds, who are also Sunni but are culturally different. They dominate in northern Iraq.

Oil, the Shah, and the Ayatollah

The conquest of much of the Middle East during the colonial era by European powers and Ottoman Turks redrew national and ethnic boundaries drastically. Two World Wars further changed the region, with many Middle Eastern nations gaining their independence afterward. The major powers, however, such as Great Britain, the United States, and the Soviet Union, were maneuvering to gain and maintain access to huge supplies of Middle Eastern oil.

After World War II, Iran's political situation was unstable. Various forces within the government disagreed on how Iran should handle its vast oil resources and which allies should benefit from them. In the end, the pro-American rule of the Iranian monarch, Mohammad Reza Pahlavi, the shah of Iran, won out.

The shah instituted Western-style changes, such as giving women the right to vote and a controversial modernization plan. While Iran's great oil wealth gave the nation and its leader great power, opponents of the regime were brutally suppressed. Thousands of political opponents were jailed. Many people feared Iran's secret police, SAVAK (Sazeman-e Ettela'at va Amniyat-e Keshvar, which is Persian for "National Intelligence and Security Organization"). SAVAK was believed to use torture, murder, and assassinations in its attempt to quell opposition to the shah. It also had

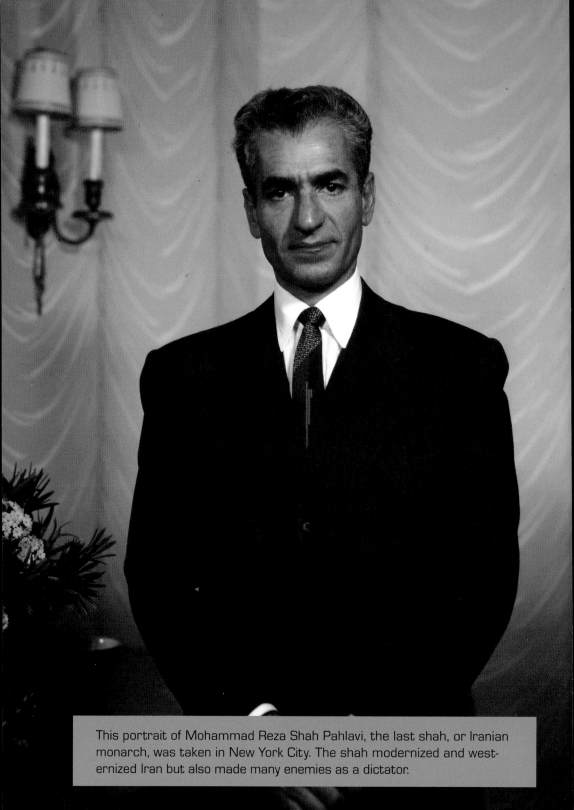

This portrait of Mohammad Reza Shah Pahlavi, the last shah, or Iranian monarch, was taken in New York City. The shah modernized and westernized Iran but also made many enemies as a dictator.

many spies and informants planted at all levels of Iranian society.

At the same time, an Islamic fundamentalist movement was growing in many Muslim nations of the Middle East. In Iran, there was an increasingly radical Islamic movement developing against the shah. This movement was very critical of Western influences in Iran and what it viewed as anti-Muslim actions by the shah's regime.

The Islamic Revolution

The central figure in the struggle against the Iranian monarchy was Ayatollah Ruholla Khomeini. The ayatollahs are high-ranking religious leaders in Shia Islam. Many of the shah's actions—increased rights for women and redistributing the property of the clergy, for example—were denounced by conservative Islamists. After Khomeini denounced the shah, his subsequent arrest sparked riots throughout Iran. The revolutionary ayatollah was eventually sent into exile in 1964. But his moment would come fifteen years later.

Khomeini spent most of his exile in Najaf, Iraq, one of the most sacred cities to the Shia. Ali ibn Abu Talib, cousin and son-in-law of Muhammad and considered by the Shia to be the first rightful successor to Muhammad, is entombed there. During this time, Khomeini quietly published works that argued for the installing of an Islamic government in Iran. He also produced cassette recordings of his speeches that were smuggled into Iran and that further helped expand the revolutionary movement. His vision of establishing a radical Shia

11

government in Iran alarmed Iraq as much as it did the shah. Khomeini was forced out of Iraq in 1978 by Saddam Hussein, who was then vice president of Iraq and was less than a year from rising to the presidency.

The revolution in Iran is considered to have officially begun in January 1978. The 1970s had seen a number of unpopular moves by the shah, including the institution of official one-party political rule and economic changes that caused high unemployment and corruption. The stage was set for massive changes in the region's greatest power. The shock waves would be felt around the world.

Iraq and the Iranian Revolution

Iraq's governments, especially that of the late dictator Saddam Hussein, have often accused Iran of meddling in Iraqi affairs. This was true especially after Iran's 1979 Islamic Revolution, when a Shia theocracy (a government controlled by religious leaders) led by Ayatollah Khomeini took control of the government.

Hussein alleged that fundamentalists loyal to Iran were trying to destabilize Iraq. His ruling Baath Party controlled a secular government, and it feared that a popular Islamic revolt could sweep through Iraq, just as it had in Iran. In addition, most of the favored government positions in Iraq belonged to Sunnis. Shia were tolerated, though many of their religious practices, such as gatherings at and processions to sacred sites, were forbidden. The Shia in Iraq often faced difficulty in Hussein's regime, even though they were more

Followers ecstatically greet the Supreme Leader of the Iranian Revolution, the Ayatollah Ruholla Khomeini *(center)*, shortly after his triumphant return to Tehran in 1979 following the ousting of the shah.

numerous than the Sunnis. Iran's Shia awakening threatened to upset the balance of power next door.

At the Brink of War

When Ayatollah Khomeini came to power, Saddam Hussein's regime in Iraq had good reason to be afraid. While Hussein ruled over a Muslim nation, his Baath political party, which had been in power since 1968, believed in socialism and secularism.

Khomeini's Shia-based movement, however, hoped to export theocracy throughout the Muslim world. Hussein considered Khomeini an enemy and a serious threat. Shia Muslims were often denied top positions in Iraq's government and had their religious freedoms suppressed under Hussein. He worried that Islamic fundamentalism would spread to his own people, threatening his power. Khomeini had urged Muslims to revolt throughout the region, especially against the Iraqi regime, which he considered anti-Muslim. *Time* magazine reported that Khomeini had even hosted Iraqi Shia leaders shortly after his return to Iran, telling them, "What we have done in Iran we will do again in Iraq."

From 1979 on, there was a renewal of border disputes between the two countries. Hussein was eyeing the important Shatt al-Arab waterway and the border province of Khuzestan. This province was important to Iran due to its strategic location, its large oil deposits, and its status as a historical seat of Persian power. He thought that Iran was weakened by internal problems arising out of its revolution. For Hussein, it seemed like a perfect opportunity to strike.

The War Years: Iraq Invades Iran

On September 22, 1980, the Iraqi military invaded Iran, with the bulk of its forces entering Khuzestan. At first, it seemed that Hussein had figured correctly: the Iranian military, once a power in the region, suffered from organizational problems and a lack of proper equipment. Within the year, Iraqi forces had occupied a sizeable piece of Iran's border regions. Many Arab (and largely Sunni) nations in the region helped Iraq

Iraqi troops man positions along a road in Khorramshahr, Iran, as pipeline fires smoke in the distance behind them. This was part of Iraqi attacks on Iran's oil infrastructure early in the Iran-Iraq War.

with money, aid, and weapons. They, too, feared the influence that Iran might wield over their own minority Shia populations.

By May 1982, however, Iran was pushing back, scoring many victories and reclaiming all of its invaded territories. By the end of June, Hussein's forces were retreating back into Iraq and forming defensive positions at the border. Hussein's Arab allies, who had supported Iraq during the invasion, offered to pay reparations to Iran as part of a peace settlement. Iran refused. With its recent victories, Iranian morale was high, and Khomeini felt emboldened. He decided to invade Iraq to depose Hussein and overthrow the Baathists.

War of the Cities, War of the Tankers

The Iran-Iraq War caused devastating losses on both sides. Once Iran had gained the upper hand, the war became a stalemate for most of the 1980s. Each side dug huge trenches in the earth and attacked each other, killing many enemy soldiers but gaining little ground. Another tactic was the "war of the cities," in which both nations attacked the cities of the other, either with bombing raids or rocket attacks. These attacks resulted in heavy civilian casualties. In the "war of the tankers," Iran and Iraq also tried to attack each other's oil shipments on the waters of the Persian Gulf.

The battlefields claimed more and more Iraqi and Iranian lives. Iran, in particular, made use of great numbers of poorly trained volunteers, new to military life but inspired by the ideals of the Islamic Revolution. Many of these men would be killed when sent in massive "human-wave" attacks against the better-equipped and more professional Iraqi forces. Iraq was implicated in several incidents of chemical weapon attacks against Iranian fighters and civilians. Some of these chemical weapons were sold to Iraq by the United States.

In the End, a Stalemate

By the late 1980s, the war had seemingly exhausted both nations, including their respective leaders. The human toll was massive: as many as one million were killed, with many more wounded. Each nation suffered

The Battle of al-Qadisiyah

The Battle of al-Qadisiyah, one of the defining moments in Islamic history, took place near present-day Hilla in Iraq in 637 CE. At that time, the Euphrates River was a natural boundary between Arab conquests and the land of the Sassanid Persians. A Persian army of up to 100,000 crossed to the western side of the river and battled against a much smaller Arab force (perhaps 30,000).

Despite initial Persian success, the Arabs overcame their foes after a few days and pushed eastward, farther into Persian territory. They took Ctesiphon, one of the Sassanids' most important cities. Within a few years, the Arab forces had defeated the Persians, extending the Muslim caliphate from North Africa to central Asia. Following the Arab conquest, Persia's largely urban population converted to Islam, some people more quickly than others. By the sixteenth century, during the Safavid dynasty, Shia Islam was the official state religion of Iran.

During the Iran-Iraq War, Saddam Hussein often portrayed the modern conflict in terms of this ancient battle between Arabs and Persians. In fact, he commissioned a monument of two hands crossing swords to be erected in central Baghdad near his presidential complex in 1990. Called the Swords of Qadisiyah, and also the "Hands of Victory," they are a reminder of this ancient divide between the neighboring peoples of Iran and Iraq.

economic pains due to the destruction of buildings and industry. Oil production was especially hard hit.

There was resentment in Iran as well, due to the support that many nations, directly or indirectly, provided to Iraq during the conflict. This resentment grew following the international, U.S.-led effort to liberate the nearby Persian Gulf state of Kuwait when Iraq invaded it two years later. No nation had offered Iran similar help when Hussein's forces had invaded it. Many observers feel that Iran's efforts to develop a nuclear program in later years were inspired by this sense of isolation and American antagonism.

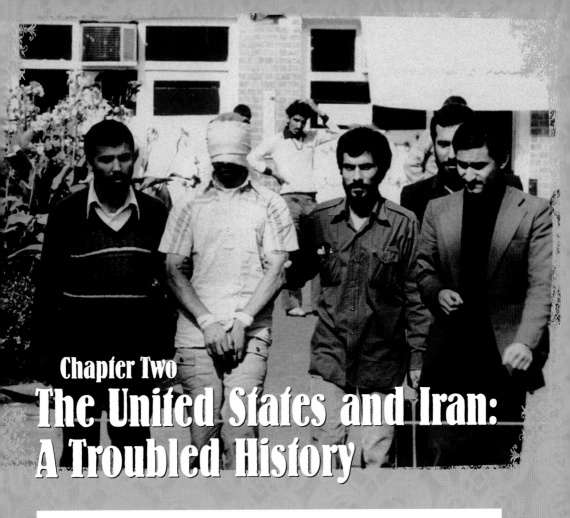

Chapter Two
The United States and Iran:
A Troubled History

L ong before the 9/11 terrorist attacks and the
ensuing war on terror, the Ayatollah Ruholla
Khomeini was the "face of radical Islam" for much of
the world. Since the Islamic Revolution, several U.S.
presidential administrations have had their run-ins
with Iran. Iran has also harshly criticized the United
States as an imperial power, sometimes declaring it
the Great Satan.

A blindfolded American hostage is displayed by his captors for the cameras
during the Iranian hostage crisis, which began in 1979. As Iran intended,
the 444-day crisis was a major embarrassment for the United States.

U.S. president George W. Bush gives his "axis of evil" State of the Union address on January 29, 2002, as Vice President Dick Cheney *(left)* and Speaker of the House Dennis Hastert look on.

Khatami and his fellow reformers felt betrayed by the "axis of evil" speech. His vice president, Mohammad Ali Abtahi, later told PBS's *Frontline*, "The very least expectation we had, at the height of our struggles for real reform, was not to be branded like this . . . That was Mr. Bush's biggest strategic and political blunder."

Bush believed that talking tough would inspire the opposition in Iran, but it seemed to backfire. The *Christian Science Monitor* reported in January 2003 that many Iranians, even young, pro-American ones, were completely perplexed by Bush's comments. Khatami's attempt to rebuild relations with the United States would become a political liability for his reform movement. Later, he would lose control of the presidency, making way for a more conservative, hard-line successor.

On the Eve of War

In the months leading up to the American-led invasion of Iraq, officials of the United States, Iran, and the Iraqi opposition were busy trying to establish what exactly would replace Saddam Hussein's regime. Toppling Hussein was one issue on which Iran and the United States saw eye-to-eye. Hooshang Amirahmadi, of the American-Iranian Council, told PBS's *Frontline* in 2007, "Iran wanted Saddam Hussein overthrown. That was absolutely 100 percent."

Amirahmadi's access to both American and Iranian officials allowed him to witness one particular exchange between Javad Zarif, Iran's ambassador to the United Nations, and Zalmay Khalilzad. Zarif told Khalilzad, who was then a member of the U.S.'s

National Security Council (NSC), that Iran needed to play a big role in the postwar era. Amirahmadi quoted Zarif as saying, "Listen, you really need our help. Let us get in with you because after Saddam leaves, the place will be a mess."

The Iranian desire to cooperate with the American invasion of Iraq was mainly due to self-interest. On one hand, the Iranians knew the region well and understood the complicated loyalties and conflicts of the Sunni and Shiites in Iraq. Deposing the much-hated Hussein was a long-standing desire of Iran. It was also in Iran's best interest to keep any tensions on its border from turning into a full-scale conflict. On the other hand, as Amirahmadi pointed out, cooperating with the United States would be one way to make the Americans think twice about turning their military on Iran once the operation in Iraq was completed.

Rise of the Conservatives

Once again, however, mutual suspicion soured any hope of warmer U.S.-Iranian relations.

Iranian president Mahmoud Ahmadinejad tours a heavy water plant in Arak, Iran, a facility that will service a nuclear research reactor built in defiance of continuing U.S. and United Nations opposition.

In fact, a window of opportunity may have closed when Mohammad Khatami, first elected in 1997, left the presidency. Khatami's hopes for democratic reforms and better international relations were strongly resisted by conservatives in the clergy and government. He also lost credibility when relations with the United States did not improve despite his best efforts, especially after Iran was included in Bush's "axis of evil."

By 2005, the conservative elites in Iran were set to reclaim the presidency. Mahmoud Ahmadinejad, a staunch conservative who had most recently been the mayor of Tehran, became president. Ahmadinejad would soon prove more confrontational with the United States and its Western allies, especially over Iran's nuclear program.

The Nuclear Question

No other issue has inspired as much tough talk between Iran and the United States as Iran's quest for nuclear technology. Publicly, Iran has declared its program "peaceful," designed only to produce much-needed energy for the country. Ayatollah Khamenei, Iran's Supreme Leader and the successor to Khomeini, who died in 1989, even issued a fatwa, or religious opinion. The fatwa declared that seeking or building nuclear weapons was anti-Islamic. Still, the United States, the United Nations, and the International Atomic Energy Agency (IAEA) have pushed Iran to abandon its program. American officials fear that Iran seeks nuclear weapons to threaten Israel and other nations in the region.

Khamenei and Ahmadinejad have firmly refused to compromise over Iran's attempts to enrich uranium. Many regional experts believe that Iran is being defiant because it thinks that possessing nuclear power will deter (or help prevent) U.S. attacks against the country. While Iran may have benefited from U.S. military action against Iraq, it was obviously becoming nervous about the large and likely long-term American military presence in neighboring Iraq and Afghanistan.

Ahmadinejad made the West even more anxious in October 2005, when he addressed a conference called "A World Without Zionism." (Zionism is the political movement that established and now supports the Jewish state of Israel.) During his speech, the Iranian president famously said that Israel "should be wiped off the map." Despite claims of peaceful nuclear power development, hostile words directed at Israel have not helped calm international fears about Iran's nuclear intentions.

Chapter Three
Iran and Its Iraqi Exiles

I t is a little-known fact that many Iraqis actually fought alongside Iranians during the Iran-Iraq conflict. Many of these Iraqis were Shia exiles who had fled to Iran after that nation's Shia-dominated Islamic Revolution. Others followed once the war started. The seeds of modern Iranian influence in Iraq were sowed when Iran took an active role in arming these Islamic insurgents.

Iraqi Shiites await Ayatollah Mohammed Baqir al-Hakim under the watch of Iranian border guards. Al-Hakim, head of the Supreme Council of the Islamic Revolution in Iraq, was returning to Iraq after a twenty-three-year exile.

The Iraqi Opposition in Iran

On one hand, the Iran-Iraq War had stirred nationalist emotions in Iraq. The historical divide between Iraqis, an Arab people, and their Persian neighbors was a real one. On the other hand, Saddam Hussein's fears of Iraqi Shia sympathies for their Iranian counterparts were not entirely unfounded. Before and during the war, there were Iraqis who identified more with their Shia neighbors than with Hussein's Baath regime, which had oppressed them for years.

Al-Dawa Al-Islamia ("The Islamic Call" in Arabic), or simply Dawa, was a Shia political party that had struggled to replace the secular Baathist regime with Islamic rule. It was often suppressed by the Baathists, who closed down many of its schools and publications. Its members were often arrested and jailed. Its gatherings were attacked, including traditional Shia religious processions.

Dawa members worked politically, waged small armed attacks, and attempted the assassination of Baath figures. The results were often harsh reprisals on Dawa members and on the Shia in general. By the time of the Islamic Revolution, openly supporting Dawa in Iraq had become punishable by death. Dawa's members were vocal supporters of the revolution in Iran and fled to Tehran, the capital city of Iran, in 1979.

The Supreme Council of the Islamic Revolution in Iraq (SCIRI)

A larger organization, the Supreme Council of the Islamic Revolution in Iraq (SCIRI), included Dawa

Ayatollah Mohammed Baqir al-Hakim gives a speech during a welcoming ceremony in Basra on May 10, 2003, barely two months after the U.S.-led invasion that overthrew Saddam Hussein, whom he had long opposed.

and other groups. SCIRI was established with substantial Iranian support and was led by Ayatollah Mohammed Baqir al-Hakim. Al-Hakim and Grand Ayatollah Mohammad Baqir al-Sadr, who was executed by the Hussein regime in 1980, were two of the most important spiritual leaders for Shiites in Iraq. They had worked together against the Baathists in the 1970s.

SCIRI, Dawa, and other groups drew membership from large numbers of Iraqi exiles in Iran. These included military officers and soldiers who had defected from Hussein's armed forces, both before and during the Iran-Iraq conflict.

The Badr Brigade

In 1982, SCIRI formed a military wing of its party, which it called the Badr Brigade (also known as the Badr Corps). The Badr Brigade was reported to be closely tied to and supported by Iran's Islamic Revolutionary Guard (IRG). Ayatollah Ali Khamenei, in his former role as president, was reported to have overseen its formation.

After Iraq was pushed out of Kuwait during the American-led "Operation Desert Storm" in 1991, Shia rebels in Iraq's south were encouraged to revolt against Saddam Hussein by then U.S. president

Armed Badr Brigade militia members march in the southern Iraqi town of Kut. The march was in commemoration of those who died in a coalition air strike in 2003.

George H. W. Bush. The Shiites hoped to take advantage of the Iraqi military's crushing defeat at the hands of the United States and its coalition allies. Badr forces made it into Iraq, while Dawa and SCIRI agents also took part in trying to inspire the rebellion.

However, coalition forces pursuing Iraqi troops within 150 miles (241 kilometers) of Baghdad were soon ordered to stand down and withdraw. Coalition leaders wanted to avoid excessive loss of life among their forces. The Badr forces and Iraqi Shia rebels, who had been counting on promised U.S. help, were soon defeated by Iraqi armed forces and Hussein's elite Republican Guard. A brutal crackdown on the Shia was waged in the following weeks. Thousands were killed and many more were forcibly relocated. It became one of the biggest disappointments for the anti-Hussein opposition. Many Shiites considered it a betrayal by the United States, opening a wound that would shape anti-American attitudes years later.

Possibility for Collaboration

Longtime suspicions and old wounds would compete with the common goals of both Iran and the United States on the eve of the Iraq War in late 2002. Though still suspicious of the Bush administration after their country was included in the "axis of evil," Iranian officials soon realized that a U.S.-led invasion of Iraq was inevitable. So, they began preparations for the postwar era.

The United States also realized that it needed Iran's cooperation if it was to wage war in Iraq and

occupy the nation following the planned overthrow of
Saddam Hussein. Officially, both nations were hostile
to each other. In fact, Iran officially declared it was
opposed to an invasion and that it would accept only
sanctions and other peaceful means to effect regime
change in Iraq. However, a mutual desire to get rid of
Hussein and stabilize Iraq opened up opportunities for
cooperation. An unnamed Iranian analyst pointed out
in an interview with the *Christian Science Monitor* that
the United States would have to get over a "deep lack
of trust, [but that] this could be another opportunity to
get together."

Iraqi exiles in Iran also weighed in. SCIRI leader
Ayatollah Baqir al-Hakim told the *Christian Science
Monitor*, "We agree with the Americans in the goal, but
our way is different. We don't want the innocent to be
killed, and we want to preserve the integrity, independence, and infrastructure of Iraq . . . But if the matter is
invasion of Iraq, or appointing an American ruler in
Iraq . . . we can't cooperate with them." A European
diplomat pointed out that while prominent mullahs still
denounced the United States publicly, cooperation would
most likely happen "as long as it is not high-profile, so
they can continue to chant 'Death to America.'"

A Reality Check for the United States

As the prospect of an invasion of Iraq grew in late 2002,
two important meetings took place. In December 2002,
around three hundred delegates—Sunni, Shia, Kurd,
Christian, activists, and the heads of nongovernmental
organizations (NGOs)—gathered in London, England,

Attendees of the Iraqi Opposition Conference in London, England, are shown here on December 14, 2002, several months before the U.S.-led invasion of Iraq. Longtime opponents of Saddam Hussein gathered to figure out Iraq's future.

to find common ground on Iraq's immediate future. Zalmay Khalilzad represented American interests at the meeting. He was in charge of collecting members for an advisory council. He found that none of the Iraqi Shia groups would finalize their council selections until they contacted Iran. In the end, SCIRI negotiated its way into fifteen out of sixty-five seats on the council.

Even more revealing were the activities of these same Iraqi Shia representatives the week before. They had gathered in Tehran to coordinate their actions at the London conference. While Iran's

Velayat-e-Faqih: "Guardianship of the Jurist"

In addition to Iraqi militants, some of Iraq's Shia clergy also took refuge in Iran. There, they were exposed to the Islamic Republic's unique philosophy of government. Many became close to their fellow ayatollahs and mullahs in the city of Qom. Iran's Islamic elite had long studied there, establishing the religious rules that governed the Islamic Republic. Qom is nearly as important a center of power in Iran as the capital city Tehran is. It is the largest center of Shia learning in the world, attracting tens of thousands of seminarians (religion students) from all over the world.

The system that the ayatollahs established is based on Velayat-e-Faqih, or "Guardianship of the Jurist." The jurists, who make, interpret, and enforce laws, are members of the Islamic clergy. Iranian law is based on sharia, or strict Islamic law, and the clergy holds a great deal of power. Thus, the Supreme Leader of the Ayatollahs is superior to the president and other branches of government in Iran. He can override decisions by secular leaders in Iran if he feels they go against Islam or the principles of the Iranian Revolution.

influence was a given, the degree to which Iraqi Shia opposition groups were taking direction from Iran was perhaps surprising—and frustrating—to the U.S. envoy. As a former State Department adviser told PBS's *Frontline*, "U.S. officials weren't happy about it, but there was nothing they could do . . . That was the bitter pill that they had to swallow. That was the reality check."

A car hit by U.S. fire burns near the shrine of Imam Ali in the holy city of Najaf, Iraq. Posters of the militant Shia cleric Muqtada al-Sadr hang in the foreground.

as well. In Baghdad and elsewhere, Shiites and Sunnis turned on each other. Murders sparked revenge killings, and the atmosphere of "eye for an eye" escalated. Shia anger over Sunni attacks would push the Shiites leadership to unite politically and militarily. Iraqi Shiites would also begin depending more heavily on Iran in the coming years of the occupation.

The Bombing of al-Askari Mosque

One of the biggest Shia campaigns against Sunnis occurred in response to the bombing of the sacred al-Askari Mosque in Samarra, Iraq, on February 22, 2006. Foreign Sunni fighters belonging to Al Qaeda in Iraq were widely blamed.

Over the coming weeks, Sunni mosques were attacked. Hundreds of Sunnis died in ambushes and outright combat in cities and towns across Iraq. Grand Ayatollah Ali al-Sistani, an influential Shia cleric, called for calm, even as he called upon the Shiites to beef up security at their houses of worship. In Tehran, Grand Ayatollah Khamenei also declared that Shiites should not take revenge against fellow Muslims. True to form, he placed direct blame upon the United States and Israel for somehow orchestrating the tragedy.

The prospect of widespread Shia unrest was a major setback for the United States. One of its aims in overthrowing Saddam Hussein was to decrease Iranian influence in the region by creating a strong democracy in Iraq. Now, it seemed that the main power brokers in Iraq had extensive ties to Tehran. Iranian influence had only grown stronger as the war dragged on.

The Mahdi Army

At the same time, groups formerly suspicious of Iran may have been establishing closer ties with it. Since the American occupation of Iraq began in 2003, it seemed that the least likely candidate to receive Iranian support was one militia leader from Baghdad, the Shia cleric Muqtada al-Sadr. He had formed the Shia militia known as the Mahdi Army in 2003. Though fiercely anti-American and violently opposed to coalition and Iraqi security forces, al-Sadr was also suspicious

A member of Muqtada al-Sadr's Mahdi Army stands guard next to a poster of the renegade Shia leader in Najaf. Meanwhile, negotiations continued to end fighting between U.S. forces and Mahdi militia members.

and critical of Iranian influence in Iraq. Nevertheless, since he is not a high-level theologian, he relies on an Iranian ayatollah based in Qom, Ayatollah Kazem Husseini Haeri, for spiritual guidance and political legitimacy.

After the al-Askari bombing, Muqtada al-Sadr ordered his militia not to seek revenge, even commanding them to help guard Sunni mosques. For him, it was a question of Iraqi national unity.

Al-Sadr draws his support from many places in Iraq, including from a Baghdad slum. The slum, called Sadr City (formerly Saddam City), is where as many as two million Shiites reside. In April 2004, al-Sadr and his

Mahdi Army clashed with coalition forces in several Iraqi cities after his newspaper, *al-Hawza*, was closed down. After his operations were suppressed by U.S. and Iraqi forces, al-Sadr made a move to disband the Mahdi Army. Instead, al-Sadr now claimed that he hoped to channel his power into politics. Yet al-Sadr's supporters and former militia members continued their violent activities.

According to a report by the United States Institute of Peace, al-Sadr, a self-described Iraqi nationalist, was initially reluctant to deal with Iran. He only became closer with Iran after realizing that he needed more weapons following his failure to beat U.S. forces in Najaf. As a result, he made a very public mission to Tehran in early 2006.

Recent Clashes

It is not always clear where Iran's support lies, or who is receiving the majority of Iranian backing at any one time. In public, official Iranian statements seem to condemn al-Sadr, especially during conflicts that arose in 2008.

By March 2008, a ceasefire existed between the Mahdi Army and its rivals: a united front of the Badr Brigades, Iraqi national forces, and U.S. troops. According to a *Guardian* report, the United States initiated raids in Basra to capture renegade fighters that they claimed were taking orders from Iran. Al-Sadr insisted that these raids were mainly aimed at his followers. In response, he began an armed campaign that month in Basra, as well as in Sadr City.

A December 2006 meeting in Baghdad's secure Green Zone brought together Iraqi prime minister Nouri al-Maliki *(center, head of table)* and tribal leaders from Sadr City, who pledged to support him.

This rebellion became a test of authority for Iraq's prime minister, Nouri al-Maliki. An Arab Shia, Iraqi nationalist, and a leader of the Dawa party, al-Maliki had been critical of the militias. Only recently, however, did it seem that Iraqi forces had grown large and strong enough to hold their own against al-Sadr's group.

After much bloodshed, al-Sadr grudgingly called for a ceasefire with Iraqi forces, which reclaimed areas of Basra in the following weeks, according to an April 21, 2008, report from the *International Herald Tribune*. Iran's ambassador to Iraq, Hassan Kazemi Qumi, publicly applauded al-Maliki's efforts and called al-Sadr's followers "outlaws."

Farther north, however, in the Sadr City neighborhood of Baghdad, Iran officially opposed U.S. actions against the Mahdi Army. Observers explain this seeming contradiction by pointing out that Iran has different aims in different areas. Baghdad is a Sunni-majority city where a large Shia militia like al-Sadr's may provide a temporary benefit to Iran's interests.

By exerting influence on many of the different Shia players in Iraq, Iran hopes to play a stronger hand than the Americans and benefit from the chaotic situation. When al-Sadr entered politics and commanded his fighters to remain inactive, some defected and splintered into smaller militias, which the U.S. suspects are being courted by Iran. As one U.S. intelligence official told the *New York Times* in September 2006, "They're not sure who will come out on top, so they fund everybody."

Chapter Five
Iran and the Rise of the Shia

I n October 2008, Iraq was set to hold another round of elections. Who would emerge the victor and how all the other parties react would be crucial in determining the nation's short-term prospects and long-term future.

On the Same Side

The United States and Iran have some common goals in Iraq. Amongst the number of Shia political parties

Islamic Supreme Council of Iraq (ISCI) leader Sheik Abdul Aziz al-Hakim has his hand kissed after leading prayers at ISCI's Baghdad headquarters.

(and their militias), both countries are giving the bulk of their support to the most mainstream group, the Islamic Supreme Council of Iraq (ISCI). This is the new name for the SCIRI as of May 2007. The name change partially symbolized the victory of an Islamic-style system over the old Baathist one.

The ISCI's leader, Abdul Aziz al-Hakim, heads this party, which holds the largest number of seats in Iraq's Council of Representatives. He used to lead the ISCI's militia and the Badr Brigades, and he is close with both the United States and Iran.

American officials have gravitated to the ISCI and the Badr Brigades because they have never attacked coalition forces during the occupation, unlike the Mahdi Army. The ISCI is also seen as the best hope to form an Iraqi government that is friendly with the United States. But they also criticize the ISCI's Iranian ties and some of its objectives.

"Shiastan"

Compared to Baghdad and the north of Iraq, southern regions have a much smaller American presence. The Sunni/Shia bloodshed of the north is not a problem here, as Shia dominate the population. Basra, in effect, is already run by the Shia in an uneasy alliance of Shia militia leaders and clerics. The ISCI and other groups hope to create a Shia zone made up of the eight southern provinces of Iraq, which they predict would be autonomous (self-governing). Such a zone would hugely benefit the Iranians, who have already established close ties there.

A large crowd of Shiites enjoy *iftar*, the dinner that breaks the day-long fast during each of the forty days of the holy month Ramadan, in Najaf, Iraq.

Opponents of this plan include many U.S. officials, as well as prominent Iraqi Sunnis. Anti-Iran hardliners argue that creating such a zone is, in effect, giving away southern Iraq to Iran. Sunnis complain that all that would remain in their possession would be the dusty provinces of central Iraq. The Shiites would control the areas with the most oil fields and access to the Persian Gulf (the port city of Basra).

Proponents of secular government, as well as women's rights supporters, are also up in arms about the creation of a "Shiastan." Basra and other southern towns were once known for social freedoms and cosmopolitan nightlife. Now, under the influence of strict Shia clergy, many areas have alcohol bans and force women to wear hijabs, or headscarves, among other strict Islamic rules.

Spreading the Wealth

Iranian money poured into southern Iraqi provinces for reconstruction and infrastructure projects. Iran has gained much goodwill in the south for supporting and funding oil and gas pipelines, electrical power generation, and road-building projects. Iranian consumer goods and money have made Najaf and Karbala arguably more prosperous than Baghdad.

Prominent Iranians, such as Ayatollah Muhammad Ali Taskhiri, have done their part, too. Professor Vali Nasr, writing for the magazine *Foreign Affairs*, claimed that Taskhiri is an influential member of the Qom clergy and is a confidant of Ayatollah Khamenei. His

Construction workers toil on a newly built bridge in Najaf on May 25, 2008. Much money for these kinds of projects has poured into the Shia south from Iranian and Iraqi Shiites after years of neglect by Saddam Hussein's regime.

Ahl al-Bayt Foundation, based in Najaf, has invested millions of dollars in the construction of medical facilities and other projects, while fostering business and culture connections between Iran and Iraq.

Along with economic influence, Iran has also extended its political and military influence in Iraq. While this concerns the United States, many observers point out that Iraqi Shiites do no necessarily want to replicate the Iranian Islamic Republic in Iraq. British-based scholar Hassan Abdulrazak pointed out to Globalsecurity.org in 2003 that Iraqi Shiites are mostly rural dwellers who belong to Arab tribes. For this reason, local tribal concerns are more important than forming a national government where Islamic clergy have all the power. Iraqi Shia parties, such as the ISCI, officially declare that the formation of a clergy-dominated Islamic republic ruled by sharia is not their goal.

Still, U.S. policymakers fear that Iranian influence in Iraq is growing too strong and will be bad for American interests. Before the invasion, they had hoped to set up a government that would be pro-American. Now, they find themselves forced to deal with Iran when trying to shape the future national government of Iraq, since Iran has become an indispensable partner in maintaining stability among the Shiites.

Grand Ayatollah al-Sistani: The Cautious Moderate

The most influential Shia cleric in Iraq, Grand Ayatollah Ali al-Sistani, was also one of the most cooperative with the United States. Born in Masshad, Iran, he has lived in Najaf since 1952. Recognizing Iraq's multi-religious makeup, al-Sistani has long opposed Iran's "guardian-ship of the jurist" as a model for Iraqi government. He has even criticized the Iranian regime on certain occasions. In addition, he has echoed many Iraqi clerics, Sunni and Shia, who feel that clergy should not be political leaders.

Al-Sistani declared in April 2003 that Shiites should not interfere with coalition military actions. One of his accomplishments was the peaceful reception of U.S. troops in Najaf, thus preventing the destruction of holy sites and bloodshed. According to the Middle East Report

Shiites hoist an image of Grand Ayatollah Ali al-Sistani during a demonstration and march from Kufa to nearby Najaf. Dozens were killed and wounded when demonstrators clashed with Iraqi National Guards.

Jafari attend a high-level meeting in Egypt weeks later. At the meeting, Jafari ignored a question about EFPs. Instead, according to *Frontline*, he pointed out that "70 percent of the terrorists captured in Iraq are from an Arab country that is a friend of the United States. To this day, not one Iranian terrorist has been captured. Not one suicide bomber has been Shia. But the propaganda is all directed against Iran. Why?" He added, "If Iran didn't help, Iraq would not have a political structure in place today."

Secretary Rice, in an offer almost like Iran's "Grand Bargain" of 2003, then told the Iranian delegation, "If Iran is prepared to accept the obligations that have been placed upon it by the international community, we are prepared, the United States, to change twenty-seven years of policy and engage with Iran on a broad range of issues, whatever is on anybody's mind." It was indeed a big reversal, especially from a top-level American official. The extending of such a dramatic offer illustrated Iran's leverage in Iraq. Clearly, Iran had gained enormous influence over Iraqi politics and governance as the war entered its fifth year.

Chapter Six
The Road Ahead

A s of late 2008, the United States remained in a
strange position regarding Iranian influence
in Iraq and America's initial aims for the region.
According to a report from the influential London-
based think tank Chatham House, "There is little
doubt that Iran has been the chief beneficiary of the
war on terror in the Middle East. The United States,
with coalition support, has eliminated two of Iran's

Members of a local neighborhood patrol Awakening Council watch over
the Adhamiya Sunni district north of Baghdad. The councils were formed
by the United States by hiring Sunnis who agreed to turn against Al
Qaeda insurgents.

regional rival governments—the Taliban in Afghanistan in November 2001 and Saddam Hussein's regime in Iraq in April 2003—but has failed to replace either with coherent and stable political structures."

Both the United States and Iran were approaching their next moves carefully. For the United States, the key would be to reduce its military might at the right time, when Iraqi forces were strong enough to stand up to militias and other threats without the benefit of backing by American troops and military leadership. The United States wanted to leave with a government in place in Iraq that will have friendly relations with it.

The worst-case scenario, besides the rise of a strict, Islamic, anti-American government, would be an all-out civil war between the Shia and Sunni. An American withdrawal in the middle of a full-scale civil conflict would be a huge undertaking. Hundreds of thousands of troops—and many more civilians, contractors, and support staff, plus all the equipment used over the previous five years—would have to be safely taken out of the country very quickly.

Meanwhile, one of the greatest challenges that faced Iraqi Shia leaders was how to include Sunnis and Kurds in a government while keeping their own supporters happy and not provoking more violence amongst the Sunnis, who felt that they were being swept aside in Iraq.

An Uncertain Future

Iran's aim is to maintain and possibly increase its regional power, with Iraq being a crucial part of its

A decrease in sectarian violence has allowed some displaced families to return to their homes. An Iraqi soldier helps register a woman returning to the Ghazaliyah area northwest of Baghdad.

strategy. If it continues moving in the same direction it has been for several years, then Iran can use its strong influence over Iraqi political parties and armed groups in many ways. For example, it can provide stability and hold together its Shia coalition, using "soft power," or diplomacy.

But it may also use its influence to threaten the United States. For example, if the United States attacks Iran's nuclear power sites or invades its territory, coalition forces in Iraq could be sitting ducks if Iran uses all its means to provoke attacks on them. Since it is unknown if or how deeply the Quds Force or other Iranian agents have penetrated Iraqi groups, it is a large risk for the United States to antagonize, much less attack, Iran while U.S. forces remain in Iraq.

Aside from a U.S. invasion of its territory, Iran's greatest fear is the emergence of a newly nationalist Iraq, much like the old Saddam Hussein regime. Such a regime may challenge it down the road or again declare war against it. Iran has few real friends among the Sunni nations in the Middle East and the larger Arab world. In fact, Iran fears that many Middle Eastern countries might be inclined to support anti-Iranian extremists next door in Iraq.

Iran also worries that Iraq could completely destabilize. A full-scale sectarian war or a failed state where lawless Sunni and Shia terrorist groups roam freely could destabilize the entire region and spill over across Iran's borders. It is a danger that the leadership in Tehran would like to avoid at all costs.

Iraq, Iran, and the United States have much to gain in the coming months and years in Iraq—and a great deal to lose. Of course, the Iraqis have already lost a great deal and continue to risk losing the most. Despite the pain that they have endured, however, it may be the Iraqis themselves who will be instrumental in bringing together the United States and Iran for the common good—building a new Iraqi nation and bringing longtime regional hostilities to an end.

GLOSSARY

ayatollahs The highest-ranking theologians in Shia Islam, they are considered leaders and experts to their followers.

Baath Party The Iraqi political party, led by Saddam Hussein, which ruled Iraq before the U.S.-led invasion.

EFP Short for explosively formed projectile, this is a deadlier type of improvised explosive device (IED) specifically made to pierce armored vehicles.

fatwa A religious declaration or opinion issued by a high-ranking Muslim cleric.

guerrilla warfare Fighting waged by irregular volunteer soldiers who are not in a formal army or state-sponsored militia; it often features sneak attacks, ambushes, and bombings behind enemy lines.

IED Short for improvised explosive device, this device is better known as a roadside bomb; an unconventional explosive device.

insurgent Someone who is rising up and revolting against an established authority.

militia An army composed of citizen soldiers rather than professional fighters, usually called up in a time of emergency.

mujahideen Meaning "holy warriors," it originally referred to the guerrilla fighters that fought the Soviet Union during its occupation of Afghanistan during the 1980s.

mullahs Muslim clerics, usually referring to Shia clergy who preside over a local mosque or particular area.

sharia Refers to a legal system based on Islamic principles.

Shia One of the two main branches of Islam worldwide, in which followers believe that the prophet Muhammad selected his son-in-law and cousin, Ali ibn Abu Talib, as the first of his proper successors.

Shiite A follower of the Shia branch of Islam.

soft power Refers to using diplomacy, rather than military action, to achieve political aims.

Sunni The dominant branch of Islam worldwide, whose followers believe in the historical succession of leaders after the death of the prophet Muhammad. Also, a follower of the Sunni branch of Islam.

theocracy A government ruled by religious leaders or that is based on religious beliefs.

Velayat-e-Faqih Meaning "guardianship of the jurist," it refers to the Iranian governing philosophy in which religious leaders and councils hold a great deal of power.

FOR MORE INFORMATION

International Society for Iranian Studies
University of California–Irvine
4800 Berkeley Place-South
Irvine, CA 92697
(949) 824-0406
Web site: http://www.humanities.uci.edu/
    iranian-studies
This organization is dedicated to Iranian and Persian
    issues. Its activities include conferences, research,
    and a journal.

Iranian Oral History Project
Center for Middle Eastern Studies
Harvard University
38 Kirkland Street
Cambridge, MA 02138
(617) 495-4055
Web site: http://cmes.hmdc.harvard.edu/research/iohp
Harvard University's Center for Middle Eastern Studies
    offers a comprehensive collection of personal
    accounts of modern Iran.

The Iraq Study Group
United States Institute of Peace
1200 17th Street NW
Washington, DC 20036
(202) 457-1700
Web site: http://www.usip.org/isg
This is a bipartisan group established by the U.S.
    Congress to analyze events in Iraq.

Iraqi Embassy
3421 Massachusetts Avenue NW
Washington, DC 20007
(202) 742-1600
Web site: http://www.iraqiembassy.us/home.htm
The Iraqi Embassy "serves as a link between the
     Republic of Iraq and the government and people
     of the United States of America," according to its
     Web site.

Mission of the Islamic Republic of Iran to the
     United Nations
622 Third Avenue
New York, NY 10017
(212) 687-2020
Web site: http://www.un.int/iran
This is Iran's envoy to the United Nations. It represents
     Iran in the international community.

Toronto Initiative for Iranian Studies
University of Toronto
4 Bancroft Avenue
Toronto, ON M5S 1C1
Canada
Web site: http://iranianstudies.ca
This University of Toronto's specialized department
     covers Iran and Persian issues.

U.S. Department of State
2201 C Street NW
Washington, DC 20520

(202) 647-4000
(800) 877-8339 (toll free)
Web site: http://www.state.gov/p/nea/ci/c2404.htm
The U.S. State Department's branch of Near Eastern
    Affairs focuses on Iran, including diplomacy issues,
    human rights reports, press releases, and more.

Web Sites

Due to the changing nature of Internet links, Rosen
Publishing has developed an online list of Web sites
related to the subject of this book. This site is updated
regularly. Please use this link to access the list:

http://www.rosenlinks.com/iran/iraq

FOR FURTHER READING

Bardhan-Quallen, Sudipta. *Iran* (Nations in Conflict). Farmington Hills, MI: Blackbirch Press, 2005.

Carlisle, Rodney P. *Iraq War* (America at War). New York, NY: Facts On File, 2007.

Coleman, Wim, and Pat Perrin. *Iraq in the News: Past, Present, and Future* (Middle East Nations in the News). Berkeley Heights, NJ: Myreportlinks.com, 2006.

Egendorf, Laura K., ed. *Iran* (Opposing Viewpoints). Farmington Hills, MI: Greenhaven Press, 2006.

Graham, Amy. *Iran in the News: Past, Present, and Future* (Middle East Nations in the News). Berkeley Heights, NJ: Myreportlinks.com, 2006.

Gray, Leon. *Iran* (National Geographic Countries of the World). Des Moines, IA: National Geographic Children's Books, 2008.

King, John. *Iran and the Islamic Revolution* (The Middle East). Chicago, IL: Heinemann-Raintree, 2005.

Piddock, Charles. *Iran* (Nations in the News). Strongsville, OH: World Almanac Library, 2006.

Rivera, Sheila. *Rebuilding Iraq* (War in Iraq). Edina, MN: Abdo Publishing, 2003.

BIBLIOGRAPHY

Abedin, Mahan. "Badr's Spreading Web." *Asia Times*, December 10, 2005. Retrieved August 2008 (http://www.atimes.com/atimes/Middle_East/GL10Ak01.html).

Ansari, Ali. *A History of Modern Iran Since 1921: The Pahlavis and After*. New York, NY: Longman, 2003.

Barker, Greg. "Frontline: Showdown with Iran." *PBS Frontline*, October 23, 2007. Retrieved August 2008 (http://www.pbs.org/wgbh/pages/frontline/showdown).

BBC News. "Iraqi Exiles Plan Path to Power." December 17, 2002. Retrieved August 2008 (http://news.bbc.co.uk/2/hi/middle_east/2583603.stm).

Carroll, Rory. "Clerics Push for Shiastan in Southern Iraq." *Guardian* (UK), August 12, 2005. Retrieved August 2008 (http://www.guardian.co.uk/world/2005/aug/12/iraq.rorycarroll).

Clawson, Patrick, and Michael Rubin. *Eternal Iran: Continuity and Chaos*. New York, NY: Palgrave Macmillan, 2005.

Cole, Juan. "Shiite Religious Parties Fill Vacuum in Southern Iraq." Middle East Report Online, April 22, 2003. Retrieved August 2008 (http://www.merip.org/mero/mero042203.html).

Crain, Charles. "How Much Is Iran to Blame for Iraq?" *Time*, February 12, 2007. Retrieved August 2008 (http://www.time.com/time/world/article/0,8599,1588135,00.html).

Dreyfuss, Robert. "Is Iran Winning the Iraq War?" *The Nation*, February 21, 2008. Retrieved August 2008

About the Author

Philip Wolny is an author and editor with a longtime interest in Middle Eastern and Muslim affairs. His written work includes titles on Afghanistan and Islam.

Photo Credits

Cover, pp. 1, 4–5 Essam al-Sudani/AFP/Getty Images; p. 7 Library of Congress Geography and Map Division; p. 10 Bachrach/Getty Images; pp. 13, 15, 32, 58, 60 © AP Images; p. 19 MPI/Getty Images; p. 22 Paula Bronstein/ Getty Images; p. 25 Mark Wilson/Getty Images; p. 27 Atta Kenare/AFP/Getty Images; p. 30 Behrouz Mehri/ AFP/Getty Images; p. 33 © Jaafer Abed Sahib/Reuters/ Newscom; p. 36 © Peter Macdiarmid/Reuters/Newscom; p. 38 Patrick Baz/AFP/Getty Images; p. 40 Sean Smith/ Getty Images; p. 43 Ghaith Abdul-Ahad/Getty Images; p. 45 Justin Sullivan/Getty Images; pp. 47, 62, 64 Wathiq Khuzaie/Getty Images; pp. 49, 55 Ahmad al-Rubaye/ AFP/Getty Images; pp. 51, 53 Qassem Zein/AFP/ Getty Images.

Designer: Sam Zavieh; Photo Researcher: Amy Feinberg